Believe

A poetry collection by

John F Connor

Fantastic Books Publishing

ISBN: 978-1-909163-25-6
Cover Design: Paula Ann Murphy

License Notes

About John

John Connor was born in 1964 and has been writing poetry since he was sixteen. Following the death of his Mother and Father, John noticed that his poetry had changed. He wrote to give himself comfort and when he shared his words with others found his poems also gave comfort to them.

Now, with thousands of followers on Facebook and a regular spot writing poetry for a grief management site called 'Healing Hugs', John is surprised at his sudden rise to fame. His work has also appeared on the 'Words of Wisdom' site which currently has over a million followers!

A down to earth family man who dreams of going to America due to his love of 1950s music, John wants his poetry to touch the hearts and souls of those lost in grief.

This is his first collection and he hopes his poetry will inspire and comfort you in your daily lives.

John has agreed to donate 10% of the proceeds from this collection to the St Helena Hospice in Colchester, UK, a charity close to John's heart.

Lost Generation

A boy lies in the gutter,
A needle by his side,
A life so short, a last resort,
He even lost his pride.

He lived without a future,
Then died without a life,
He will never know the happiness
Of children and a wife.

A pusher makes a million,
He'll make it out of sorrow,
Another trip, another hit,
Another death tomorrow.

They say it will not harm you,
They say you'll feel no pain,
For they know once you try it,
That you'll be back again.

Many young lives wasted,
Before they have begun,
Let this be a warning,
To each and everyone.

In My Shoes

They do not understand my pain,
They say I should be strong,
They say that it's not right,
To grieve for far too long,
They say I need to get back up,
They say in time I'll heal,
But they are not the ones,
Who feel the way I feel,
Some days I want to lie in bed,
And stay there all day long,
What's the point of getting up?
What's the point? You've gone?
They say things will get better,
That time will heal my blues,
Maybe they would understand,
If they walked in my shoes.

My Dad

Dad worked hard all of his life,
He had no time for pleasure.
The moments that I had with him,
Are memories I treasure,
He always said goodnight
And placed a kiss upon my head,
Regardless of how late it was,
As I lay asleep in bed,
He was gone before I woke,
And wasn't home till late,
I wanted to be there for him,
But mum wouldn't let me wait,
I didn't want for anything,
But I'd give all I had,
Just to have a bit more time,
Together with my dad.

In a Perfect World

In a perfect world there would be no pain,
And everyone would be treated the same,
In a perfect world there would be no war,
Nobody rich, nobody poor,
In a perfect world there would be no greed,
No one would have more than they need,
In a perfect world there would be no shame,
No one out for their own gain,
In a perfect world all anger would cease,
And everyone would live in peace,
A perfect world it can come true,
In the end, it's up to me and you.

The Brightest Star

When you look at the sky tonight,
You will see a new star shining bright,
To let you know, that star is me,
I will be the brightest star you see.

There Is

There is black, there is white,
There is day, there is night,
There is weak, there is strong,
There is right, there is wrong,
There is good, there is bad,
There is happy, there is sad,
There is peace, there is war,
There is less, there is more,
There is hate, there is love,
There is below, there is above,
There is light, there is dark,
There is stop, there is start,
There is loss, there is hope,
There is cotton, there is rope,
There is me, there is you,
There is lying, there is truth,
There is run, there is walk,
There is silence, there is talk,
There's an opposite to all you do,
The choice you make is up to you.

My Garden

In this world we live such stressful lives,
Everybody needs just a little space,
When the day is done I sit in my garden,
I have built myself a special place.

I have a special chair and I sit there,
I lie back and look up to the sky,
And all my worries just drift away,
As I watch the clouds rolling by.

In my garden I escape the world,
In my garden I feel proud,
I sit there alone with all of my thoughts,
Far away from the bustling crowd.

Cherish

Cherish every second,
Every hour, every day,
Live life to the full,
Live it your own way,
Grab it with both hands,
And hold on really tight,
Just follow your dreams,
And you will do alright.

If

If today goes wrong,
Don't just sit there and cry,
There's always tomorrow,
To give it another try.

Life

Life is a book,
Written over the ages,
It's not about the cover,
But what's written on the pages.

Sister

We share a special bond,
A bond that's like no other,
Nothing can ever come between,
A sister and her brother.

Morning

When I wake up in the morning,
And I watch the rising sun,
I realise each day's a gift,
And make the most of every one.

Grief

Don't tell me to get over it,
Don't tell me to be strong,
Don't tell me time's a healer,
Don't tell me to move on,
I need my time to grieve,
I need my time alone,
No one else can rush me,
I need to do this on my own,
Yes, it may take me a while,
Yes, it may take years,
Yes, I may just shout and scream,
And cry so many tears,
But only when I'm ready,
Not because you tell me so,
For when the time is right,
I will be the one to know.

Love

I love you more than words can say,
I think about you every day,
Every day I want you to know,
Just how much I love you so.

Take a Moment

Take a moment every day,
Let your mind just drift away,
Close your eyes and think things through,
Your heart will tell you what to do.

Strength

I will not go quietly into the night,
I will stand my ground and fight,
You think I'm weak but I am strong,
I'll be standing long after you have gone.

Blue Sky

Dear moon, why so blue?
Alone up in the sky,
Not so bad, but why so sad?
As you watch the world go by,
Dear moon, what do you see?
As you look down on me,
I am alone, all on my own,
No stars for company,
Dear moon, why do you cry?
Do you feel my pain?
Tell me moon will I find love
And happiness again?
Dear moon, please stay a while,
We were just having fun,
You know it's true, I can talk to you,
I can't talk to the sun,
Dear moon, goodnight and bless,
Thanks for listening to my plight,
I think I'll sleep right through the day,
So I'll see you tonight.

Too Young

Too young to fall in love, they say,
But who are they to know?
We might be young and having fun,
In time our love will grow,
Too young to settle down, they say,
But that is not my plan,
You treat me like a boy,
When I need to be a man.
Don't grow up too fast,
Enjoy life; have some fun,
It doesn't last forever,
It could be over before it's begun,
Being young is special,
The best time of our lives,
Plenty of time in the future,
For being husbands and wives.

New Day

The sun comes up,
A brand new day,
Ready to take on,
What comes my way,
Each day's a gift,
Not to be wasted,
Life is a drink,
That has to be tasted,
Some days are good,
Some days are bad,
Some days you're happy,
Some days you're sad,
If you have a bad one,
Don't fill up with sorrow,
You just never know,
What will happen tomorrow.

Winter Nights

I am sick of winter nights,
I want to see the sun,
I want to put on shorts,
I want to have some fun,
I am sick of chilly nights,
Waking up to snow,
I want to enjoy myself,
But there's nowhere I can go,
It's dark when I go to work,
It's dark when I leave at night,
I must be suffering from SAD,
I really miss the light,
Sitting in my garden,
Drinking beer would be nice,
But my garden's covered in snow,
My patio's full of ice,
I really miss the summer,
How I wish that it was here,
I do not like the winter,
It's not my time of year.

Too Short

Life's too short to worry,
Life's too short to be sad,
Life's too short to ponder,
On things you've never had,
Life's too short for sadness,
Life's too short for tears,
Never count the days,
Never count the years,
Life's too short for falling out,
Life's too short for war,
Life's a gift, don't waste it,
Life is so much more.

Love Lost

I guess I did not realize,
The truth was written in your eyes,
The love we had has died a death,
I guess I shouldn't hold my breath,
I guess I thought our love was pure,
Now I guess I'm not so sure,
I loved you but you didn't love me,
So blinded by love, I did not see.

Think

Do you ever think about
All the things you've done?
The good times and the bad times,
The laughter and the fun?
Do you wish you could go back
And live a certain day?
Would you leave it as it was,
Or change it in some way?
You meet the girl you loved and lost,
Be given a fresh start,
The girl you really wanted,
The girl who broke your heart,
You know what you did wrong,
A chance to put things right,
A chance to make amends,
To change that curtain night,
How would it work out?
Was it meant to be?
Would you risk your future,
Just to go back and see?

What If?

What would happen if war did cease?
No more fighting, only peace,
No more worry, no more fears,
Only laughter, no more tears,
No more hunger, no more fights,
Every one with equal rights,
No one too rich, no one too poor,
Let them without be given more,
No children hurt and no more pain,
Let hot desert feel the rain,
No more sadness, only joy,
Our gift to every girl and boy,
May all of our children's tears,
Fall in a world of hope not fears.

Christmas

Christmas time and you're not here,
There is no joy, there is no cheer,
No silver bells, no Christmas tree,
All I want is you with me,
No mistletoe, no lights, no holly,
No Santa Claus to make me jolly,
No Christmas cards, no carols sung,
No pulling crackers, having fun,
No evergreen, no snow so white,
No cookies left out overnight,
No decorations hung up high,
No flying reindeer in the sky,
No children's laughter, looks of joy,
No children playing with their toys,
No TV means no repeats,
No big lunch, just empty seats,
No mistletoe or stolen kiss,
No shooting star to make a wish,
For if you are not with me here,
For me there'll be no Christmas cheer.

Take Me Back

Take me back to the place I miss,
Take me back to where I was born,
One last time to see the sunset,
One last time to see the dawn,
Let me be with my family,
The people I hold dear,
I do not want to die alone,
I want my family near,
I want to say my last goodbyes,
To the people close to me,
I'm not alone when I'm back home,
That's where I want to be.

Was it Love?

Love came and went and now it's gone,
I am wondering where I went wrong,
We had love and we had laughter,
But that was not what she was after,
She wanted things I could not give,
She couldn't live the life I live,
She wanted a big house, flashy car,
Living life like a movie star,
Me, I work from nine till five,
With overtime I just survive,
I am not rich and I'm not poor,
It's not my fault I don't earn more,
But I am happy the way I am,
It's not what you earn that makes you a man.

Goodbye

I never thought it would end this way,
Me and you with nothing to say,
Been together all these years,
Times of laughter, times of tears,
Thought what we had was true,
All I ever wanted was you,
Me, I did not need another,
You're my friend and my lover,
Now you say we've grown apart,
You want to make a brand new start,
But I don't fit in to that plan,
You've found yourself another man,
But now I cannot change your mind,
How can you be so unkind?
I wish you well in all you do,
My life is empty without you,
But I know I must be strong,
Build a new life now you've gone.

Only You

I miss you today,
I will miss you tomorrow,
Nothing can take,
All the pain and the sorrow,
In my life there's something missing,
There seems to be an empty space,
No one can ever fill it,
No one can take your place,
I love you like no other,
Right till the very end,
I didn't just lose my husband,
I lost my best friend.

In Time

Their comes a time in everyone's life,
When it's time to say goodbye,
There's no way to get away with it,
It's a fact of life that we die,
Life's a gift so do not waste it,
Make use of each and every day,
Be careful what you do to others,
Be careful what you say,
Help them who are in need,
Both the hungry and the poor,
To become a caring person,
Is what we live life for.

Something

There's something about,
The way you look tonight,
It makes me feel,
That things may be alright,
We've had our problems,
We've had a few,
But it's our love,
That helped to pull us through,
I know our love is special,
Our love is pure,
We can ride the storms,
I know that for sure,
I will always love you,
You're all that I need,
To ask for any more,
Would just be greed,
Let's take each day that comes along,
Problems help our love grow strong,
It feels so right when we're together,
We've got a love to last forever.

Just a Letter

Just had to write you a letter,
Upon this Christmas day,
I am still in our old home town,
And you're so far away,
Memories come flooding back,
Of times back in our past,
Our childhood was an endless summer,
Of times too good to last,
I remember when you moved in
To the house across the road,
I stood there at my window,
And watched the trucks unload,
I remember as your dad parked up,
And you got out the door,
I knew my heart was lost to you,
I fell in love with what I saw,
I passed you many times,
But found it hard to speak,
Till a group of us decided,
To play a game of hide and seek,

I asked you if you would like to play,
The hardest thing I'd ever done,
I had to smile when you said yes,
Oh, that day was fun,
After that we became good friends,
And spent much time together,
When I think back I wish,
It had stayed that way forever,
Time did pass and we grew up,
Together through teenage years,
We built ourselves a special bond,
Through the laughter and the tears,
I began to see you in a different way,
Feelings I could not hide,
I should have told you how I felt,
I guess it was my pride,
I watched you go out with other guys,
You even asked me for advice,
If I had a chance to hold you near,
I wouldn't think about it twice,
You said I was like a brother,
A brother you never had,

I smiled and I said thank you,
I hid the fact that I was sad,
Your future was ahead of you,
It was time to let you go,
I waved to you at the station,
It hurt more than you'll ever know,
I heard all about your life,
You would always write a letter,
My life was dull and boring,
Your life seemed so much better,
I heard that you were coming home,
But inside I was full of rage,
Your mum said that you'd met a man,
That you two were engaged,
I smiled and wished you all the best,
I even wished him well,
Outside I was putting on a brave face,
Even though I was going through hell,
At Christmas time I think of you,
I always do this time of year,
But you are far away,
And I'm the one stuck here.

Mind's Eye

Shut your eyes and open your mind,
You never know what you may find,
All your hopes and all your fears,
Memories of all those years,
A place of peace, a place of calm,
To hide away, be safe from harm,
A place of thoughts, a place of care,
A place you know is always there,
Close your eyes and open your mind,
You never know what you may find.

I Dream

I dream of peace and understanding,
Surely that's not too demanding,
I dream of a world that's free from war,
That's a dream worth waiting for,
A world without hunger, pain or fear,
Where no one needs to shed a tear,
A world of laughter, joy and fun,
A world without need to carry a gun,
Safe to walk the streets at night,
And know that you will be alright,
A world where illness has a cure,
That's a world worth waiting for,
But is my dream within my grasp?
If so can we make it last?
Let our children fear no more,
That's a world worth waiting for.

How Much

How much does for a sunset?
How much for a kiss?
How much for a smile?
How much for a wish?
How much for a mother?
How much for a dad?
How much to be happy?
How much to be sad?
How much for a blue sky?
How much for a stream?
How much for a child's love?
How much for a dream?
How much for a thank you?
How much for a please?
How much for the clouds?
How much for the trees?
Take a look around,
Look at all you see,
The best things in life are free,
I'm sure you will agree.

New Dawn

A whiff of hair,
Eyes of blue,
Out of the dark,
Into a world of new,
First breath of air,
First time to cry,
So much to learn,
New things to try,
First time you see me,
First time I see you,
So much to see,
So much to do,
Very first sunrise,
Like your life at its dawn,
But it's time to sleep,
As you give out a yawn,
Sleep well little prince,
May your dreams all be sweet,
For now I have you,
My life is complete.

Home

Sister is upstairs doing her hair,
Mum's downstairs, she's going spare,
Dad just sits there in his chair,
Watching the game, he doesn't care,
Brother is waiting for a bath,
Him? A bath? Don't make me laugh,
Since he met that girl he's acting daft,
Now he's even drinking halves,
Mum, she's busy cooking dinner,
Every time she cooks a winner,
For my mum is no beginner,
If you miss it, you're a sinner,
I love my home I really do,
When I'm away I feel so blue,
It's there for me to pull me through,
Is your home the same for you?

Hope

How come countries can't unite?
All they seem to do is fight,
Settle things with iron fists,
If they only knew the risks,
How great it would be if war did cease,
And everyone could live in peace,
All together side by side,
No one with a thing to hide.

Shame

Last night I woke up with a scream,
I had a really terrible dream,
I dreamed I was blind, I could not see,
And everyone they picked on me.

They shouted and they pushed me around,
Until I fell upon the ground,
Even then they carried on,
Although I had done nothing wrong.

If your body is not all there,
They pick you out, they look, they stare,
You feel so guilty, you feel the shame,
Even though you're not to blame.

What if it's not me, but them?
Maybe then they'd think again,
Maybe then they'd understand,
And make this place a better land.

Time

I am lost and looking for answers,
But don't know where to start,
Learning to live without you,
Dealing with being apart,
My world has been turned upside down,
I am lost and all alone,
I need to deal with this my way,
I need to do it on my own,
I need to find my own way out,
Of this dark place I am in,
I need to gather all my strength,
If I am going to win,
I need to realise that others,
Who are just like me,
Searching for the answers,
Hoping to break free,
I will not happen overnight,
This healing might take years,
There will be a lot of soul searching,
There will be a lot of tears,
But one day I will find them answers,
I'll learn to live again,
When I realise one day,
That we will meet again.

I'm Still Here

Just because you cannot see me,
Does not mean I am not there,
Just because I am in heaven,
Does not mean I do not care.
I often see you crying,
You often call my name,
I want to hold you tight,
I want to ease your pain.
It's easy for me,
For I know heaven's real,
If you knew the truth,
How much better would you feel?
One day we will meet again,
But only when the time is right,
When you step out of the darkness,
I will be standing in the light.

Letter to Mum

I see you Mum but you do not see me,
But I am always there,
I watch you when you are sleeping,
I gently stroke your hair,

I hug you when you cry,
I kiss you when you're sad,
I sit beside you as you look through photos,
Of the good times we both had,

I often say I love you,
In words you cannot hear,
I know sometimes you feel me,
You just know that I am near,

So don't cry Mum, I love you,
I have not gone forever,
Just watching over you in heaven,
Till it's our time to be together,

It is hard to watch you suffer,
Knowing there's nothing I can do,
Our bond cannot be broken,
I will help to pull you through,

Death is not the darkness,
Death is everlasting light,
Keeping me from harm,
Until my time is right.

The End

Did you enjoy this collection?

If so, please show your appreciation by telling all your friends and leaving John a review online.

Thank you for supporting John's work.

SPACE FOR **YOUR** THOUGHTS

SPACE FOR **YOUR** THOUGHTS

SPACE FOR **YOUR** THOUGHTS

SPACE FOR **YOUR** THOUGHTS

SPACE FOR **YOUR** THOUGHTS

Made in the USA
Middletown, DE
30 December 2023

46989492R00055